Traditional Animal Designs and Motifs

for Artists and Craftspeople

Madeleine Orban-Szontagh

DOVER PUBLICATIONS, INC., New York

Publisher's Note

Animals have played a vital role in the mythology and folklore of every society and culture throughout history. Gathered here is a representative selection of animal motifs from around the world, rendered in authentic traditional styles by artist Madeleine Orban-Szontagh. The artist has taken her inspiration from animal motifs found on textiles, ceramics, woodcarvings, stencils and a variety of other traditional craft forms. The drawings are arranged loosely by region: Plates 1–26 represent the Americas; Plates 27–55, Europe; Plates 56–74, Africa; Plates 75–116, the Near East and Asia; and Plates 117–126, Polynesia and Australasia.

In addition to its geographical range, however, this book has a historical dimension. Not all the designs are current or recent productions of their region. For example, much of the Latin American material is pre-Columbian; the Nigerian plates include several devoted to the art of Benin, a separate kingdom until 1897; and so on.

Copyright © 1993 by Dover Publications, Inc.
All rights reserved under Pan American and International Copyright Conventions.

Published in Canada by General Publishing Company, Ltd., 30 Lesmill Road, Don Mills, Toronto, Ontario.
Published in the United Kingdom by Constable and Company, Ltd., 3 The Lanchesters, 162–164 Fulham Palace Road, London W6 9ER.

Traditional Animal Designs and Motifs for Artists and Craftspeople is a new work, first published by Dover Publications, Inc., in 1993.

DOVER *Pictorial Archive* SERIES

This book belongs to the Dover Pictorial Archive Series. You may use the designs and illustrations for graphics and crafts applications, free and without special permission, provided that you include no more than ten in the same publication or project. (For permission for additional use, please write to Dover Publications, Inc., 31 East 2nd Street, Mineola, N.Y. 11501.)

However, republication or reproduction of any illustration by any other graphic service, whether it be in a book or in any other design resource, is strictly prohibited.

Manufactured in the United States of America
Dover Publications, Inc., 31 East 2nd Street, Mineola, N.Y. 11501

Library of Congress Cataloging-in-Publication Data

Orban-Szontagh, Madeleine.
    Traditional animal designs and motifs for artists and craftspeople / Madeleine Orban-Szontagh.
        p.   cm. — (Dover pictorial archive series)
    ISBN 0-486-27485-3 (pbk.)
    1. Decoration and ornament—Animal forms—Themes, motives. I. Title. II. Series.
NK1555.O73   1993
745.4—dc20   92-43113
                                                                                              CIP

PLATE 1. Early American.

PLATE 2. Early American.

PLATE 3. Early American.

PLATE 4. Early American.

PLATE 5. Early American.

PLATE 6. Early American.

PLATE 7. Native American: Northwest Coast.

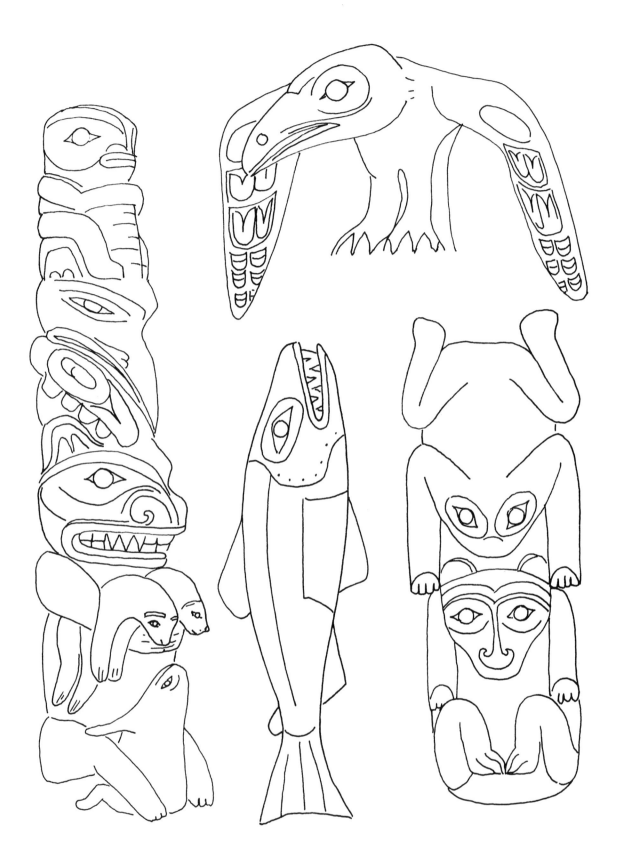

PLATE 8. Native American: Northwest Coast.

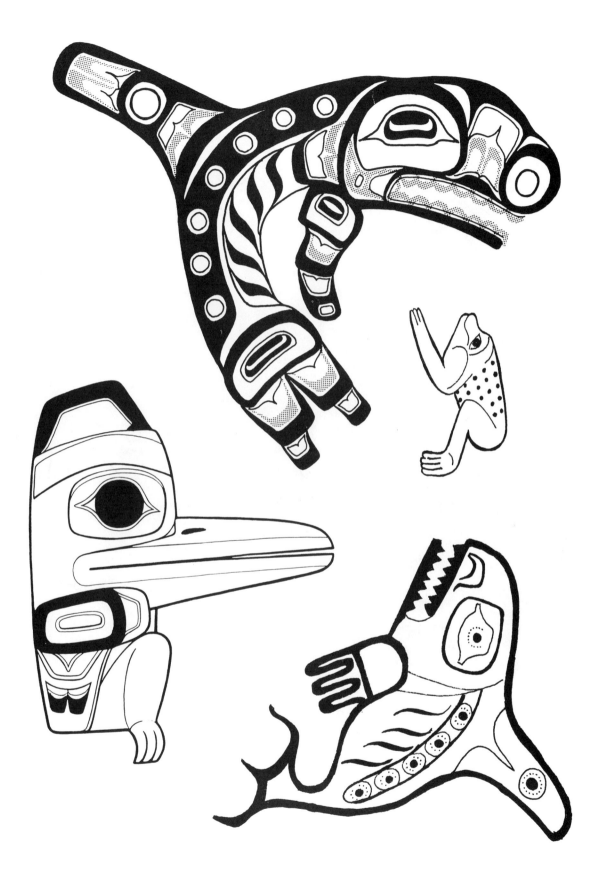

PLATE 9. Native American: Northwest Coast.

PLATE 10. Native American: Southwest.

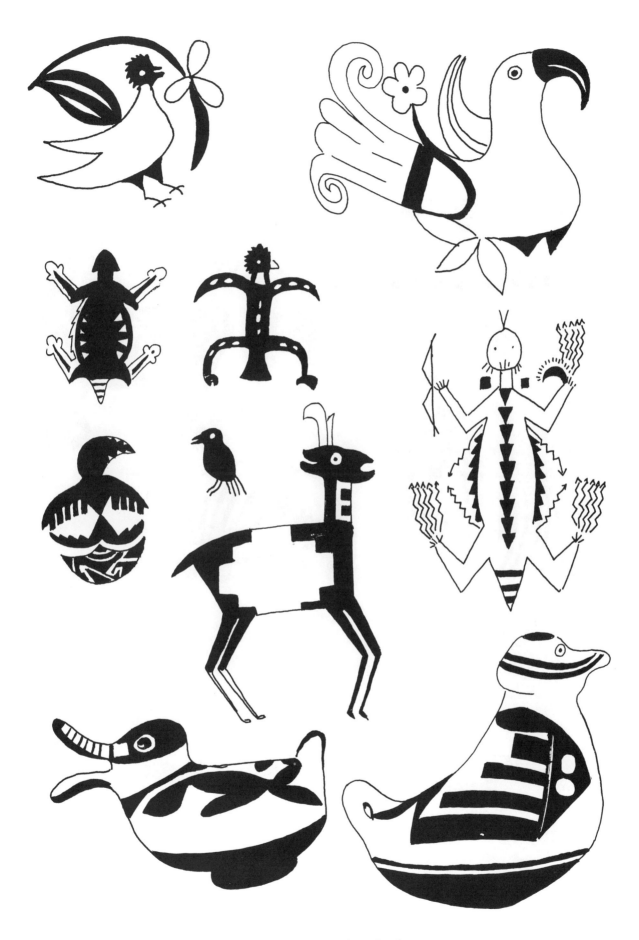

PLATE 11. Native American: Southwest.

PLATE 12. Latin America.

PLATE 13. Costa Rica.

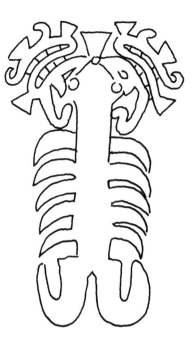

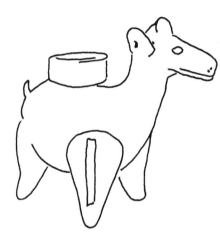

PLATE 14. Costa Rica.

PLATE 15. Costa Rica.

PLATE 16. Panama.

PLATE 17. Panama.

PLATE 18. Mexico.

PLATE 19. Mexico.

PLATE 20. Mexico.

PLATE 21. Chile.

PLATE 22. Peru.

PLATE 23. Peru.

PLATE 24. Paraguay.

PLATE 25. Venezuela.

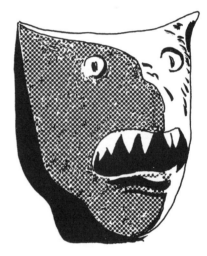

PLATE 26. Argentina.

PLATE 27. England.

PLATE 28. France.

PLATE 29. Switzerland.

PLATE 30. Italy.

PLATE 31. Italy.

PLATE 32. Italy.

PLATE 33. Italy.

PLATE 34. Greece.

PLATE 35. Greece.

PLATE 36. Germany.

PLATE 37. Sweden.

PLATE 38. Hungary.

PLATE 39. Hungary.

PLATE 40. Hungary.

PLATE 41. Poland.

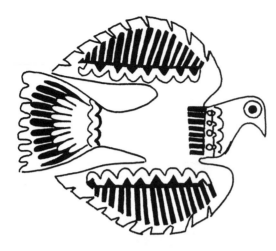 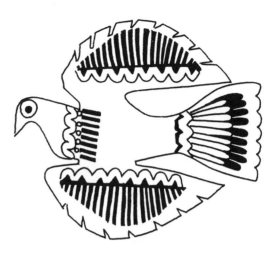

PLATE 42. Poland.

PLATE 43. Poland.

PLATE 44. Poland.

PLATE 45. Ukraine.

PLATE 46. Ukraine.

PLATE 47. Ukraine.

PLATE 48. Ukraine.

PLATE 49. Ukraine.

PLATE 50. Russia.

PLATE 51. Russia.

PLATE 52. Russia.

PLATE 53. Russia.

PLATE 54. Russia.

PLATE 55. Georgia (former USSR).

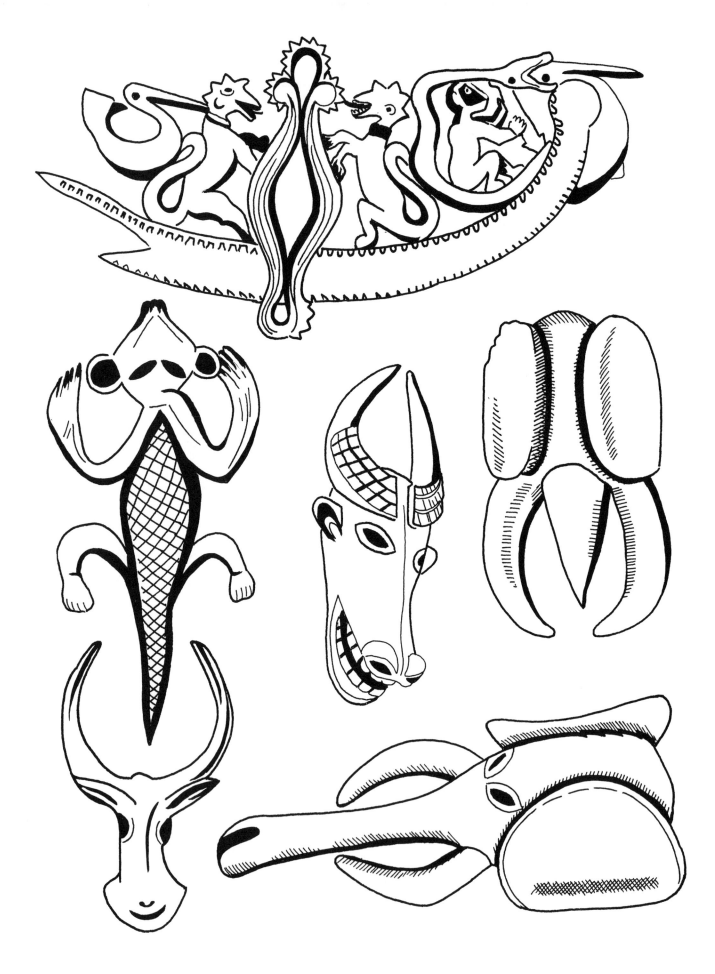

PLATE 56. Cameroon.

PLATE 57. Ghana.

PLATE 58. Ghana.

PLATE 59. Ghana, Ivory Coast.

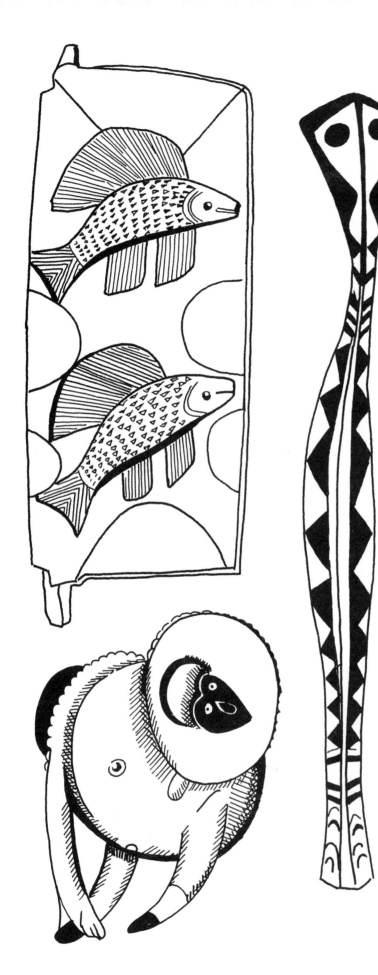
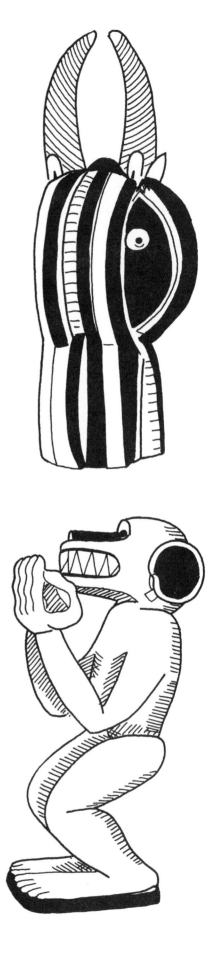

PLATE 60. Ivory Coast.

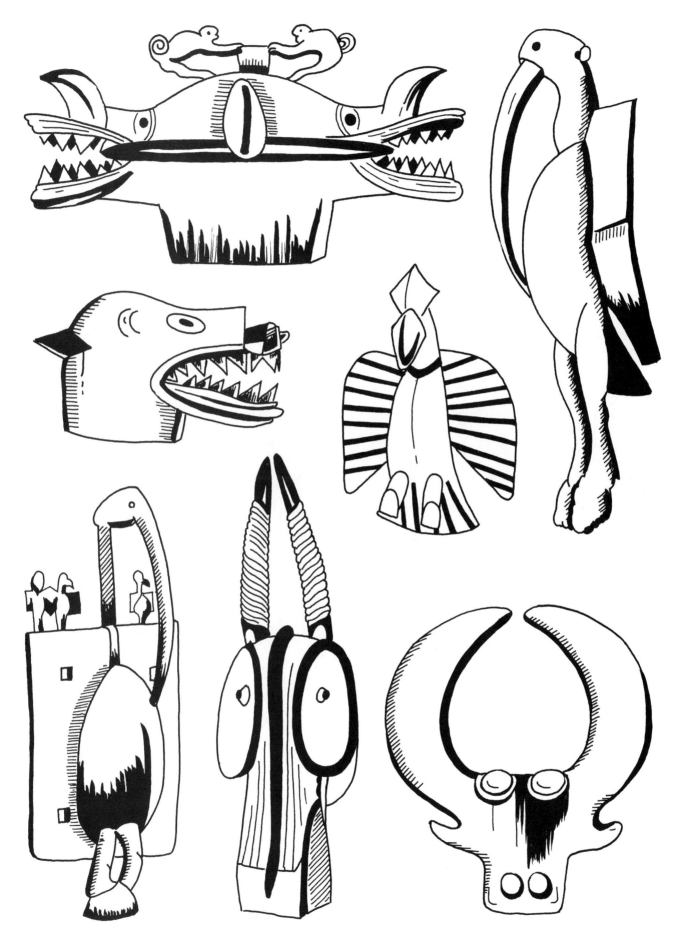

PLATE 61. Ivory Coast.

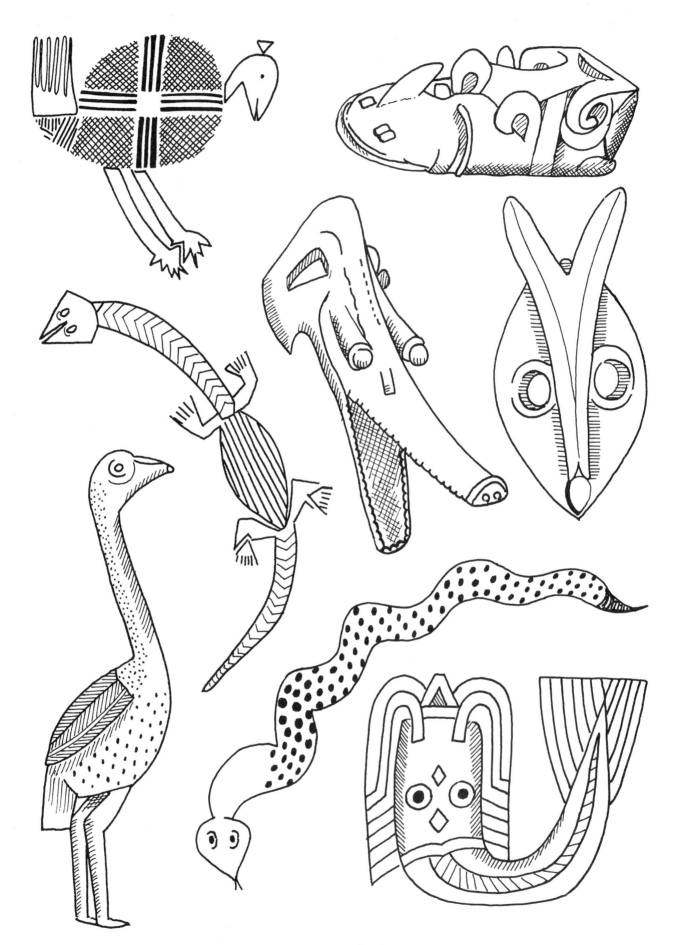

PLATE 62. Nigeria.

PLATE 63. Nigeria.

PLATE 64. Nigeria.

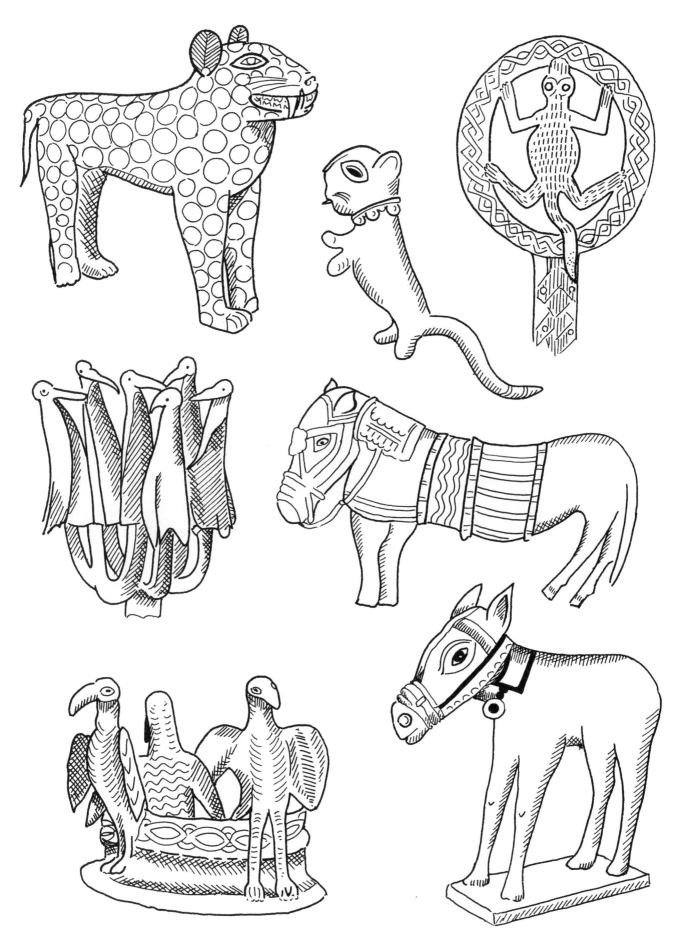

PLATE 65. Nigeria.

PLATE 66. Nigeria, Mali.

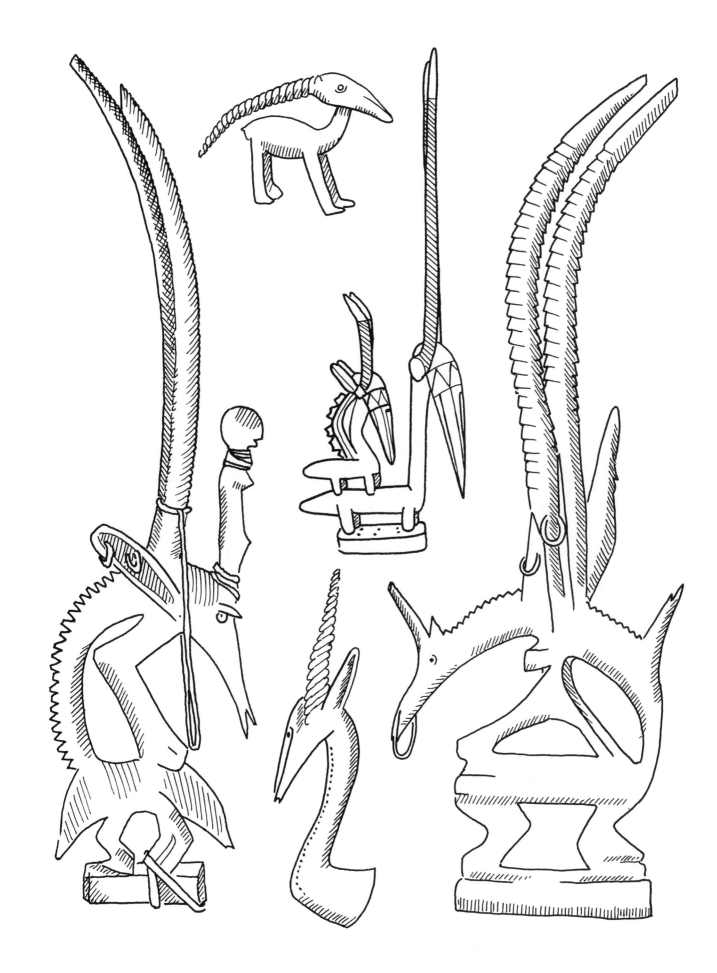

PLATE 67. Mali.

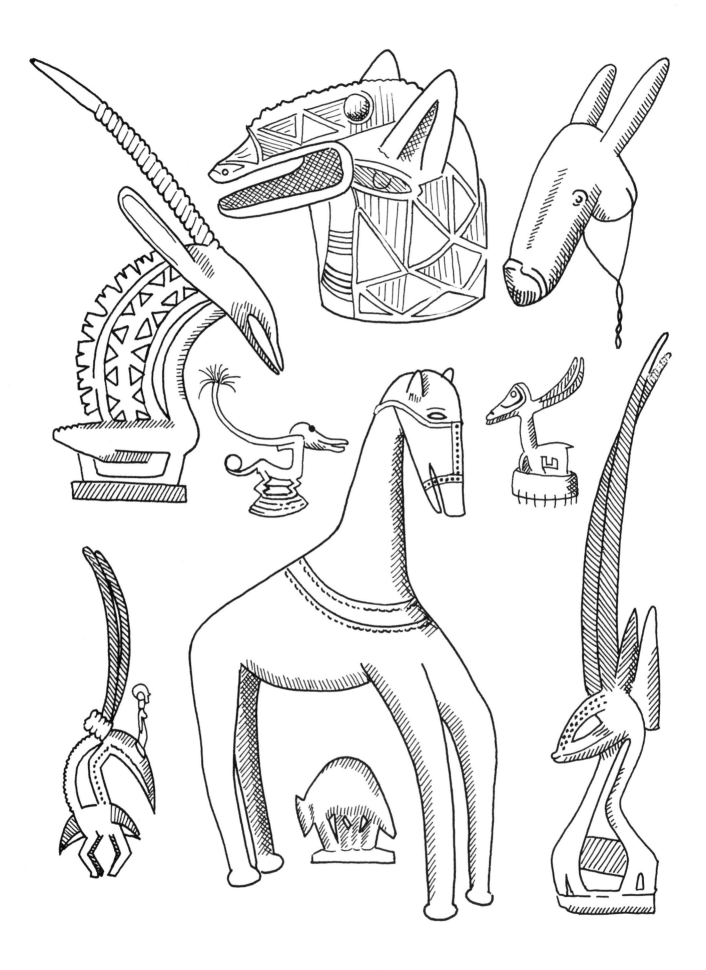

PLATE 68. Mali.

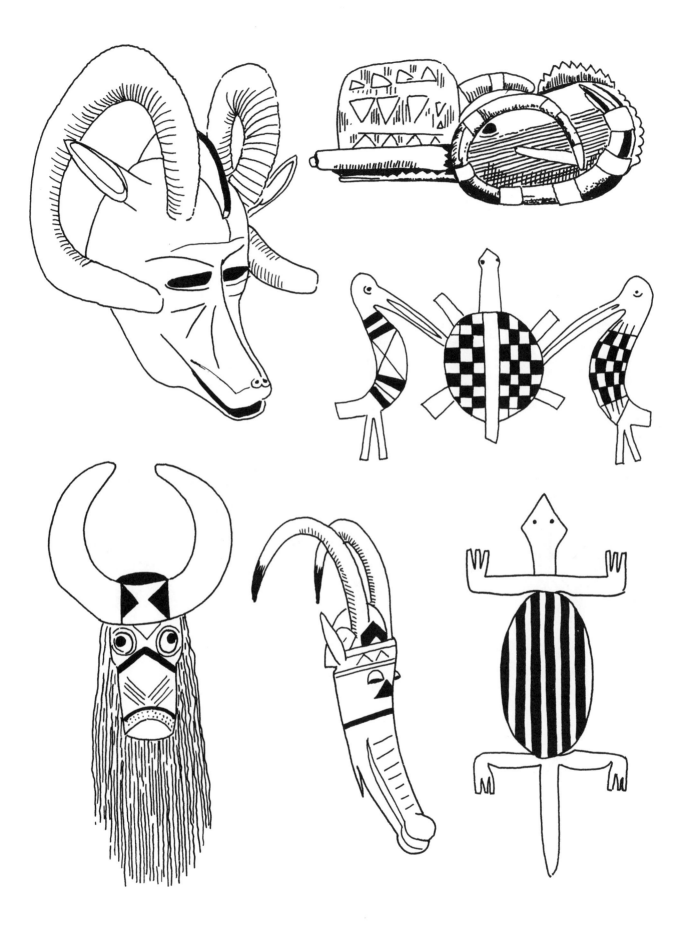

PLATE 69. Upper Volta.

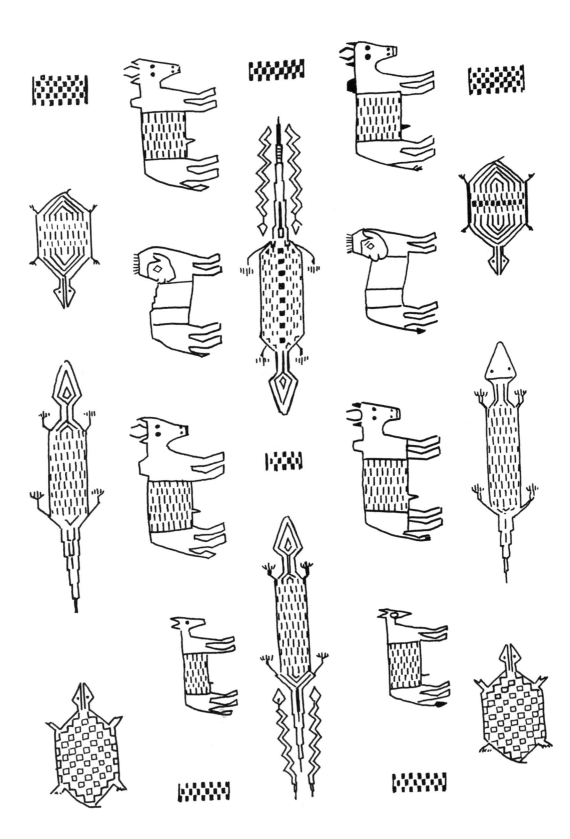

PLATE 70. Niger.

PLATE 71. Zaire, Central African Republic, Congo.

PLATE 72. Southern Africa.

PLATE 73. Southern Africa.

PLATE 74. East Africa, Zimbabwe.

PLATE 75. Egypt.

PLATE 76. Egypt.

PLATE 77. Egypt.

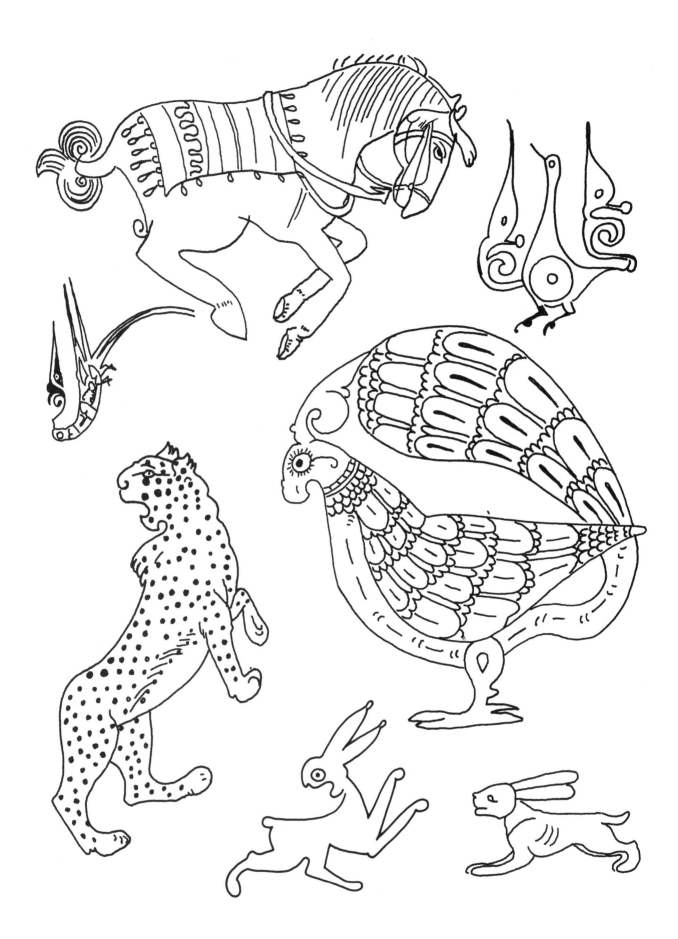

PLATE 78. Iraq, Iran.

PLATE 79. Iraq, Iran.

PLATE 80. Central Asia.

PLATE 81. Bangladesh.

PLATE 82. India.

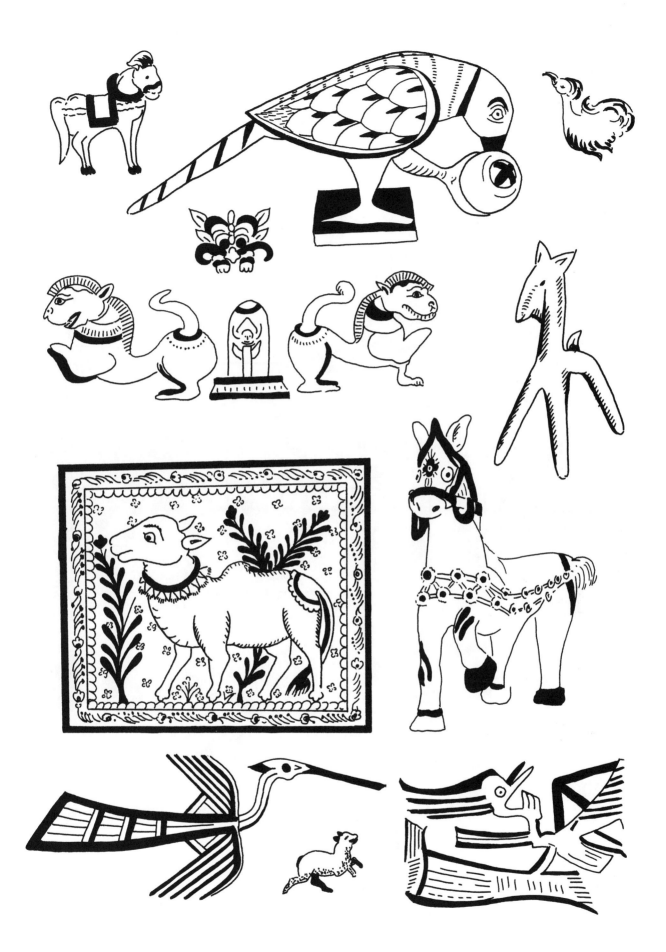

PLATE 83. India.

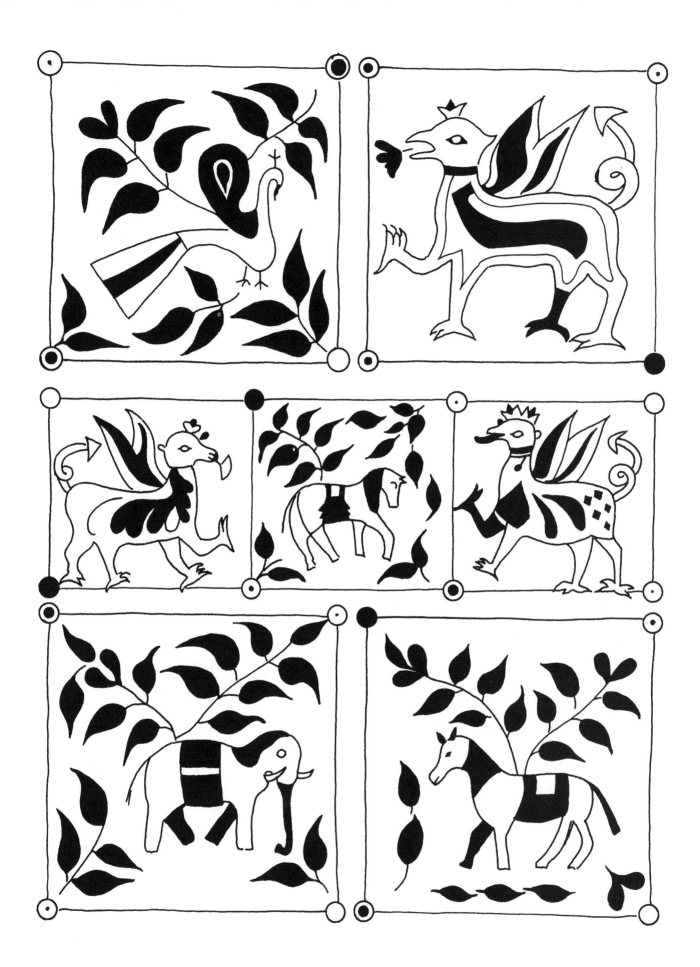

PLATE 84. India.

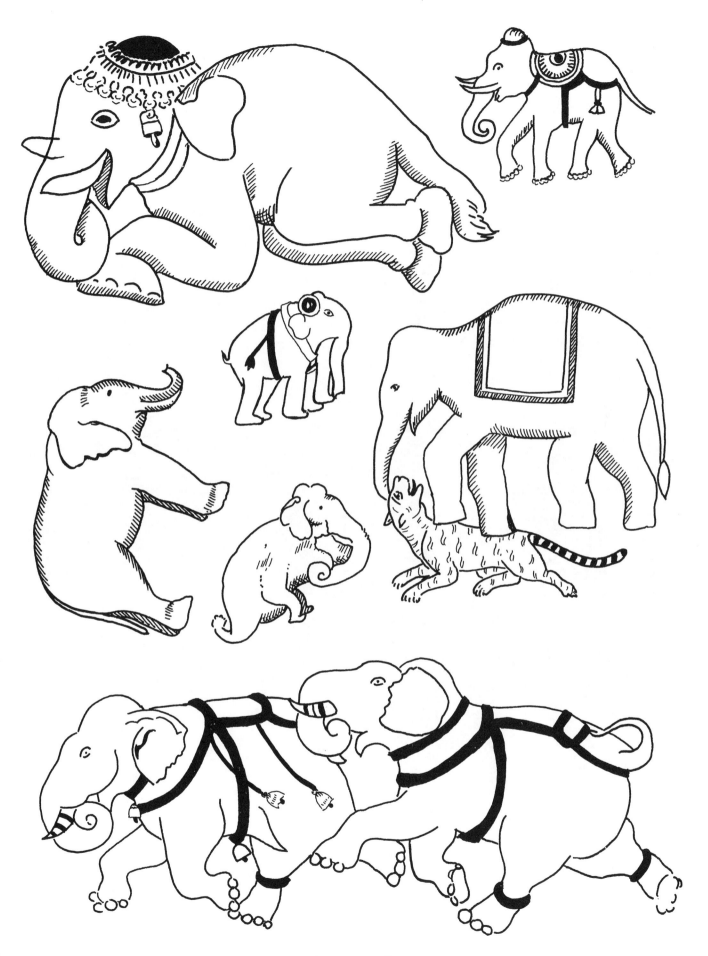

PLATE 85. India.

PLATE 86. India.

PLATE 87. India.

PLATE 88. Himalayas.

PLATE 89. Himalayas.

PLATE 90. Himalayas.

PLATE 91. Himalayas.

PLATE 92. Himalayas.

PLATE 93. Borneo (Indonesia).

PLATE 94. Borneo.

PLATE 95. Borneo.

PLATE 96. Lesser Sunda islands (Indonesia).

PLATE 97. Lesser Sunda islands.

PLATE 98. Sumatra (Indonesia).

PLATE 99. Sumatra.

PLATE 100. Bali (Indonesia).

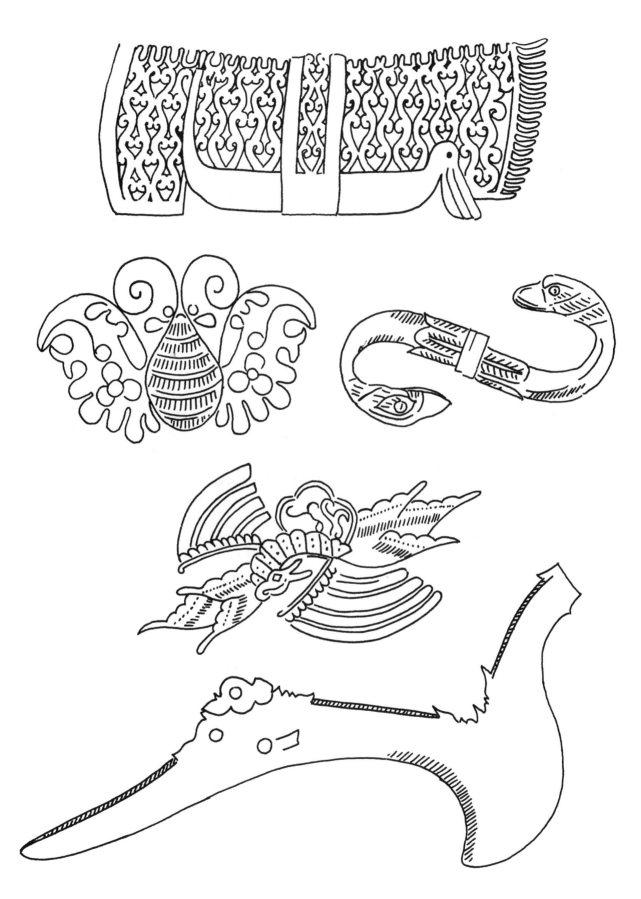

PLATE 101. Java (Indonesia).

PLATE 102. China.

PLATE 103. China.

PLATE 104. China.

PLATE 105. China.

PLATE 106. China.

PLATE 107. China.

PLATE 108. Korea.

PLATE 109. Korea.

PLATE 110. Korea.

PLATE 111. Japan.

PLATE 112. Japan.

PLATE 113. Japan.

PLATE 114. Japan.

PLATE 115. Japan.

PLATE 116. Japan.

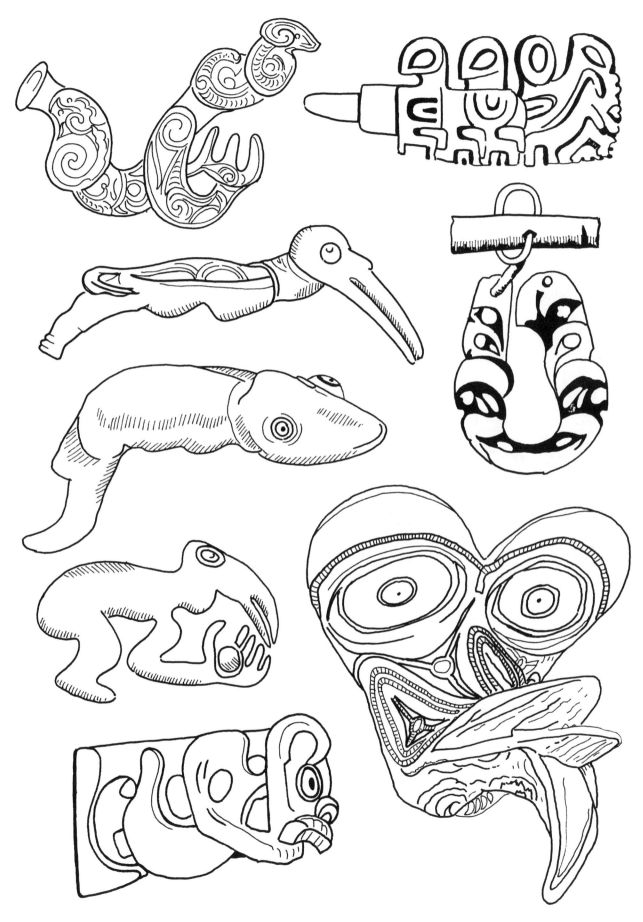

PLATE 117. Polynesia.

PLATE 118. New Guinea, New Ireland, Marianas.

PLATE 119. New Guinea, Solomon Islands.

PLATE 120. New Guinea, New Ireland.

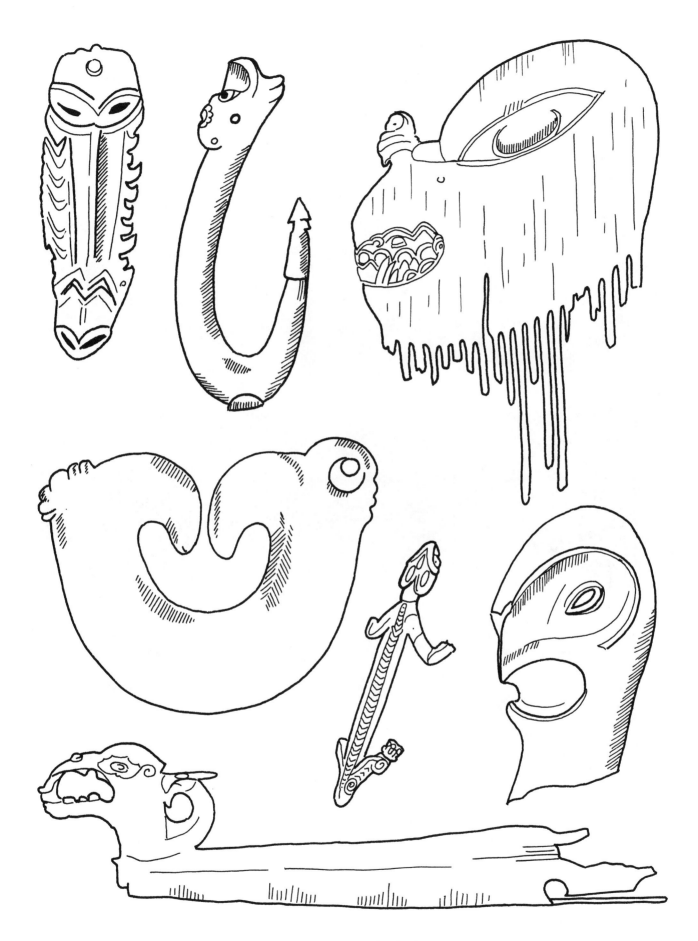

PLATE 121. New Zealand.

PLATE 122. New Zealand.

PLATE 123. New Zealand.

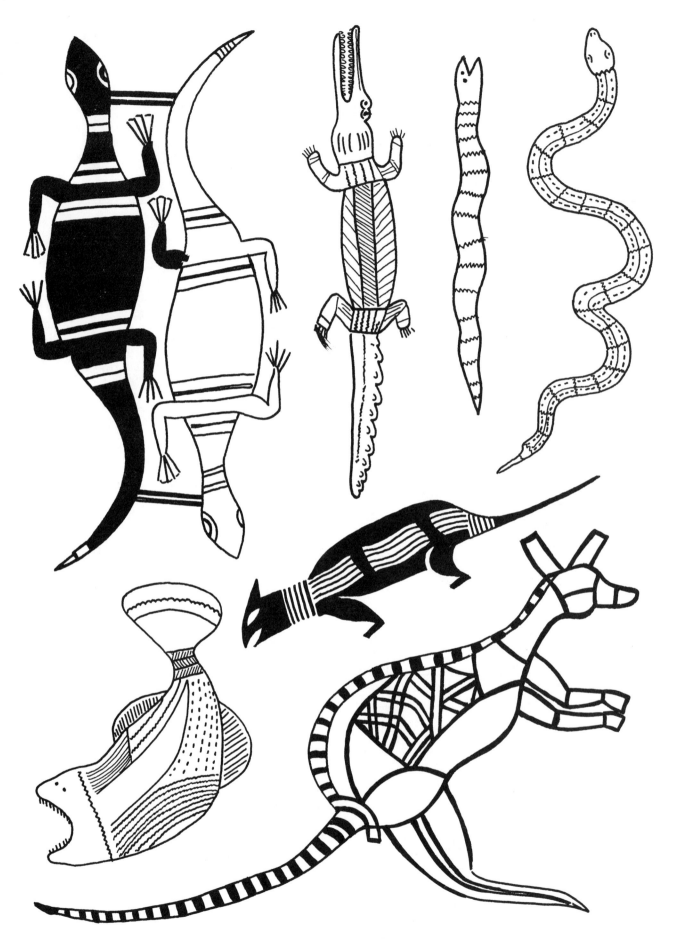

PLATE 124. Australia.

PLATE 125. Australia.

PLATE 126. Australia.